ANGELS IN OUR HEARTS

25 Reflections, Prayers, and Activities to Prepare you for Christmas

Karen Kazimer Shockley

Karen's Words

*To my children, Barbara, Julia and David, they
will forever reside in my heart.*

CONTENTS

"And suddenly there was with the angel a multitude of the heavenly hosts praising God and saying: "Glory to God in the highest, And on earth peace, goodwill toward men!""

Bible, King James Version, Luke 2:13-14

INTRODUCTION

Do you often feel like the world is turning upside down, leaving you searching for stability? In the midst of life's chaos, there is an anchor that can bring you peace—God. But God doesn't leave us to navigate this world alone; He provides us with tools like faith, hope, and love. And among these gifts are His angels, who play a crucial role in guiding and comforting us, just as they did in foretelling the birth of Christ.

In *Angels in Our Hearts*, I share my belief in these heavenly beings and explore their significance during the Advent and Christmas seasons. Through scripture, personal reflections, and real-life experiences, this book offers a spiritual journey filled with hope and inspiration. With twenty-five prayers and activities for each day of Advent, you'll find ways to prepare your heart for the true meaning of Christmas. Let the presence of angels guide you toward a deeper connection with God this holiday season.

PREFACE

Abrahamic religions (think Judaism, Christianity and Islam, although there are others) often describe angels as benevolent celestial intermediaries between God (or Heaven) and humanity. The word, "angel", literally means "messenger." In the Bible, angels usually appeared as men when they delivered messages from God to people (see Genesis 18:1-3).

The Angel Gabriel appeared to at least three people in the Bible. He interpreted a vision for Daniel (Daniel 8:16), told Zechariah about the birth of John the Baptist (Luke 1:19), and proclaimed to Mary that she would be the mother of the Messiah (Luke 1:26).

Angels are at the heart of the Christmas season. Through their words, Mary and Joseph became filled with joy and awe at the coming of the Savior in the form of their child. Angels spread the word to the shepherds in the nearby countryside. And later, angels warned of the need for a quick departure to Egypt.

ANGELS IN OUR HEARTS

Angels are in our hearts. They touch our minds and our souls. They protect us. They bring messages from God. They protect us in the battle against evil. This book focuses on angels and the celebration of Christmas. Our celebration of Christmas formally begins with Advent as we ready our hearts and minds to receive the gift of Jesus' birth.

Angels are so significant in the occurrence of this miracle that, without them, the Christmas story would be vastly different. First, there was the Angel Gabriel, who showed himself to Mary. He brought the good news that she was to bear a child.

Next, there was the angel who visited Joseph to bring not only the wonderful news that he was to become a father, but that his Son was to be the Messiah. Again, on Christmas Eve, angels attended the birth of Christ, bringing wonder and joy to the new family. Angels then shared this special news with nearby shepherds so that they might visit the newborn and rejoice in His presence. And, finally, the angels warned the Holy Family that evil was coming with sufficient time for them flee to Egypt.

BIBLE VERSES

The presence of angels in the Christmas story reminds us that Christ's birth is no ordinary event. Instead, it is supernatural; it is divine. From announcing the conception of Jesus to sharing the joy with nearby shepherds, the angels played a critical role in guiding and proclaiming the good news of salvation. The following paragraphs convey the bible verses that showcase the use of angels to spread God's Word.

LUKE 1:26-28

"Now in the sixth month the angel Gabriel was sent by God to a city of Galilee named Nazareth, to a virgin betrothed to a man whose name was Joseph, of the house of David. The virgin's name was Mary. And having come in, the angel said to her, "Rejoice, highly favored one, the Lord is with you; blessed are you among women!""

Reflection

Take a moment to place yourself in Mary's shoes. She must have been terrified. First, she was visited by an angel. Second, she was told she would have a baby. How did you react when you were given some surprising news? Would you pray to the angel in your heart?

My Story

When I first heard this bible verse as a seven-year-old child at St Bartholomew Catholic School, it frightened me. I imagined my reaction if the Angel Gabriel came to me. At my tender age, I did not wish to be anyone special. I would not have wanted to be singled out as being blessed. I wouldn't have wanted the burden of caring for our Lord. But herein lies the beauty of the angel's message. For with this message came joy and light and hope. Joy that the Lord was with Mary; the light of the Lord that bathed her in love; hope for the miraculous things to come. It is only with these three gifts that Mary would have been able to accept the angel's message. Yet these three gifts yielded a fourth: strength. Mary was also given the strength to marry, give birth to a child and love Him with all her heart.

MATTHEW 1:20-21

"But while he thought about these things, behold, an angel of the Lord appeared to him in a dream, saying, "Joseph, son of David, do not be afraid to take to you Mary your wife, for that which is conceived in her is of the Holy Spirit. And she will bring forth a Son, and you shall call His name Jesus, for He will save His people from their sins."

With these words from the angel, Joseph was thrust on the world stage of humanity. He was given the responsibility of carrying for a wife and raising a son who would become a savior for all people. Imagine, if you will, a man betrothed to be married who has just learned his wife is with child. I'm sure many thoughts went through his mind from, "why me?" to "can I really believe this angel?" To fulfill God's plan, Joseph needed to embrace the gift of a child, along with the joy, light and hope that accompanied him.

Reflection

Have there been times when a role you did not wish for was thrust upon you? Did you spend time bemoaning this special task? Did you wish that someone else would take this burden from you? I think that we all have.

My Story

I once had the opportunity to teach a mathematics class at Park College. Park College is now Park University, but it is the same institution where I taught military students' intent upon attaining their degree. So, on the one hand, this was a most wonderful place to teach. All of the students were motivated. On the other hand, part of this motivation was tied to financial considerations. Any student not receiving a C in the class would not have their tuition re-imbursed. So, as much as I hated doing so, I did award students with the "D"s they earned, knowing they could ill-afford the consequences.

When I say opportunity, think volunteered. I still am not sure exactly how I agreed to fill this post. I was in the Air Force, working at the Pentagon; my husband was also in the Air Force, stationed in Washington, DC and we had a two-month-old baby. When this opportunity arose, I had more than a full plate. It seemed to me impossible to take on this task. But I did.

And this decision became an extraordinary blessing. The students were wonderful, attentive, hard-working. I had a very real feeling that I was contributing to their lives. We became a community that celebrated together when a new student grasped a difficult concept. In addition to being a wonderful experience, the students provided an even greater opportunity. My ratings were among the highest ever received by an instructor at that school. People actually wanted to meet "the great instructor". And when I left the Air Force, I was offered a full-time job there.

I also felt very humble as one of the students who knew he was going to receive a "D" offered to provide tickets to the Marine Corps Silent Drill Exhibition. The organization featured in the show is a 24-man rifle platoon that performs a unique precision drill exhibition, silently. I did attend the show. It was spectacular. Please make the time to see it if you find yourself in DC at the appropriate time of year. While I did not take the full-time job, I taught at Park College for many years, always grateful I accepted the challenge way back when. I was very glad that the angel in my heart urged me to go forward.

LUKE 2:13-14

"And suddenly there was with the angel a multitude of the heavenly hosts praising God and saying: "Glory to God in the highest, And on earth peace, goodwill toward men!""

Reflection

Angels not only witnessed the birth of Christ and celebrated with the new family, but spread the word of happiness. It says much that they were part of this very special moment. Reflection Is there a time in your life when you feel an angel may have brought you good news? Or at least a time when good news was unexpected but very welcome?

My Story

Here is my Christmas message of joy. Me, my mom and my two daughters were standing in my mom's living room. This instance occurred approximately three months after my dad had passed away. We happened to be in front of the family creche. The same set of statues had stood in the same places on the dining room cabinet for over thirty years. This manger scene also had a battery powered candle for a light source. We were admiring the scene when my mom said, "I so wish your grandpa could be here with us". No sooner had she uttered the statement when the candle flickered, just as if my dad WAS there and was letting us know. This was a very obvious flicker. All four of us noticed and commented on it. And once again, we felt at peace knowing that my dad's spirit was among us. This message significantly brightened our Christmas experience.

LUKE 2:8-9

"Now there were in the same country shepherds living out in the fields, keeping watch over their flock by night. And behold, an angel of the Lord stood before them, and the glory of the Lord shone around them, and they were greatly afraid."

Reflection

Have you had the experience being a shepherd? That is, have you ever had the charge of protecting someone, either physically or spiritually? Parents know this charge well; they are shepherds for their children, watching over them, guiding them and keeping them safe. Children, in turn, become shepherds of their parents as they age, assuming responsibility of caretakers and providers.

My story

This story involves me and my guardian angel. I was four-years-old and diagnosed with tonsillitis. I'm not sure how things are now, but during that time it was fairly common for children with infected tonsils to have them removed. So, to follow the standard protocol, my tonsils were removed. And then, according to my parents, began a month-long recovery period. Most of this time was spent in the hospital. Something was cut that didn't heal and I continued to bleed.

Of course, I also did not eat. When you are four-years-old and your throat hurts there is virtually nothing on earth that can make you eat. Even the promise of unlimited ice cream post operation does not help. This stay must have been a fairly significant experience for me, because I still remember it.

I remember that the little girl in the bed next to me celebrated her birthday in the hospital and received a bride costume. At that time, there was nothing more that I wanted in the whole world than a bride costume. I'm sure I didn't tell my mom; an excellent seamstress, she most likely would have whipped one right up.

I remember there were nuns and an activity room. For some reason, a child could color a ready drawn picture (think of a coloring book) but it had to stay in the activity room. If, on the other hand, a child drew a picture and added color, that picture could be taken home. I'm sure there was a need to save money there somewhere, but not being able to take home the "good" pictures bothered me for years.

I also remember making a friend of a little girl with black curly hair. We decided that green Jell-O tasted like cement. This was an interesting observation since we had, to the best of my knowledge, never even eaten cement.

I also remember that my Uncle Lou and Aunt Gladys brought me three puzzles. These were the kind that had silver balls and a picture with holes in it surrounded by a plastic case. The idea was to move the case around to allow the silver balls to drop into the designated holes. I think I had those puzzles until I went to college!

But let's go back to the guardian angel. I believe that my guardian angel was bored with watching me in the hospital getting no worse but not getting better. She must have sent a message to my dad. One day, he had had enough of the hospital. He just picked me up, wrapped me in a blanket and spirited me away to another doctor. That doctor cauterized my wound and I was healed! At which time my angel could move on to other things. My dad was truly my shepherd, assisted by a messenger from God.

MATTHEW 2:13

"Now when they had departed, behold, an angel of the Lord appeared to Joseph in a dream, saying, "Arise, take the young Child and His mother, flee to Egypt, and stay there until I bring you word; for Herod will seek the young Child to destroy Him."

Reflection

This bible passage shows that angels cannot only bring joy, but they can bring warnings. This message was given to the Holy Family to ensure their safety so that greater things might ensure. Has there been times in your life when you have felt a sudden urge to act, to choose one path over another? Could this have been an angel guiding your direction?

My story

As I was about to give birth to my second child, I had several dreams during the day. These dreams concerned delivering my child at home. I could see the mat on the floor where the baby would be laid. I could know that the baby was healthy. I could feel the love around me. I know in my heart that these visions originated from a heavenly being. Unfortunately, I did not heed the message of the dreams. I could have paid attention and thus been on alert when my labor began. I could have let my birth coaches know that things might not go according to plan. I could have prepared space in my house. In reality, I did none of these things and my baby was born at home, just as I had seen in my dreams. My guardian angel, however, not only provided ample warning, but ensured that my daughter and I stayed healthy. We were bundled into an ambulance and whisked to the nearest hospital where some of the best care in the world awaited.

ANGEL CHRISTMAS SONGS

I love all Christmas carols. To me, they are an essential part of this sacred season. Even in elementary school we experienced the joy of learning carols. In fact, in fourth grade I was introduced to two- part harmony in the form of the song, "Silver Bells". I was given the privilege of singing Alto!

One year as I returned to my family home with my spouse and children, I was determined to involve everyone in singing carols. I carefully created a song book, complete with words to all of my favorite hymns and distributed them during "singing time". Not everyone in the family was attuned to this wonderful celebration event. To my disappointment, singing carols did not become an annual event. But I was not deterred forever. Many years later my two girls joined their friends, carrying songbooks prepared by one of their mothers. As a group, they carried out the time-honored tradition of singing songs to neighbors. There are special hymns, however, that evoke visions of angels. I'm sharing them with you now so that you can easily experience their joyful words. Perhaps they will assist in keeping an angel in your heart.

Angels We Have Heard on High

The lyrics of "Angels We Have Heard on High" were inspired by a traditional French Christmas carol. This carol was first named "the angels in our countryside" and was written as far back as 1842.

"Angels We Have Heard on High" is now the most common English version. This was a particular favorite of mine as a child. I sang it many times at St Bartholomew Church. I really enjoyed the "Gloria in Excelsis Deo" line because of the note changes that occur within the word, "gloria". If you are not familiar with this song, I recommend you locate a copy and listen to it. It is quite inspiring. Here are the lyrics so that you may enjoy them, too.

Angels we have heard on high

Sweetly singing o'er the plains

And the mountains in reply

Echoing their joyous strains

Gloria in excelsis Deo!

Shepherds, why this jubilee?

Why your joyous strains prolong?

What the gladsome tidings be?

Which inspire your heavenly songs?

Gloria in excelsis Deo!

Come to Bethlehem and see

Him whose birth the angels sing;

Come, adore on bended knee,

Christ the Lord, the newborn King.

Gloria in excelsis Deo!

See Him in a manger laid

Whom the choirs of angels' praise;

Mary, Joseph, lend your aid,

While our heart in love we raise.

Gloria in excelsis Deo!

The First Noel

"The First Noel" is another hymn that embodies Christmas for me. Of Cornish origin, this song was first published in 1823. It provides a magnificent rendition of the story of Christ's birth. Perhaps you can understand my delight with this song. They looked up and saw a brilliant star that foretold good news.

The First Noel the Angels did say

Was to certain poor shepherds in fields as they lay

In fields where they lay keeping their sheep

On a cold winter's night that was so deep

Noel Noel Noel Noel

Born is the King of Israel!

They looked up and saw a star

Shining in the East beyond them far

And to the earth it gave great light

And so it continued both day and night

Noel Noel Noel Noel

Born is the King of Israel!

And by the light of that same star

Three Wise men came from country far

To seek for a King was their intent

And to follow the star wherever it went

Noel Noel Noel Noel

Born is the King of Israel!

This star drew nigh to the northwest

O'er Bethlehem it took Its rest

And there it did both Pause and stay

Right o'er the place where Jesus lay

Noel Noel Noel Noel

Born is the King of Israel!

Then let us all with one accord

Sing praises to our heavenly Lord

That hath made Heaven and earth of nought

And with his blood mankind hath bought

Noel Noel Noel Noel

Born is the King of Israel!

Noel Noel Noel Noel

Born is the King

Born is the King

Born is the King of Israel!

It Came upon a Midnight Clear

Also, a favorite hymn of mine was "It Came Upon a Midnight Clear". I liked this song especially because of the presence of angels and the images it evoked of a still winter night. As I sung this as a child, I could picture a calm, clear starlit sky with the manger resting in the fields below. In my vision, Christ was born while the angels sang and the shepherds proclaimed their wonder. "It Came Upon a Midnight Clear", was introduced in 1849 as both a poem and Christmas carol. This hymn follows a different path than the normal one of relating the story of Bethlehem. Instead, its focus seems to be on war and peace, as simultaneously relaying the Christmas story. Perhaps, this song was written as a response to the just ended Mexican-American War. Read the lyrics for yourself and determine what you believe.

From angels bending near the earth

To touch their harps of gold;

"Peace on the earth, good will to men

From heaven's all-gracious King" –

The world in solemn stillness lay

To hear the angels sing.
Still through the cloven skies they come

With peaceful wings unfurled,

And still their heavenly music floats

O'er all the weary world;

Above its sad and lowly plains

They bend on hovering wing,

And ever o'er its Babel-sounds
The blessed angels sing.

But with the woes of sin and strife
The world has suffered long;
Beneath the angel-strain have rolled
Two thousand years of wrong;
And man, at war with man, hears not
The love-song which they bring; –
Oh hush the noise, ye men of strife,
And hear the angels sing!

And ye, beneath life's crushing load,
Whose forms are bending low,
Who toil along the climbing way
With painful steps and slow,
Look now! for glad and golden hours
Come swiftly on the wing; –
Oh, rest beside the weary road
And hear the angels sing!

For lo! the days are hastening on
By prophet bards foretold,
When with the ever circling years
Comes round the age of gold;

When Peace shall over all the earth

Its ancient splendors fling,

And the whole world give back the song

Which now the angels sing.

ADVENT REFLECTIONS

PRAYER FOR DAY ONE

Lord, we eagerly await the birth of your Son. Make our hearts and minds ready to know Him.

Activity

Think of ways that you can become prepared to welcome the Christ child into your heart and home. You may want to perform an extra special house cleaning reminiscent of the old adage, "Cleanliness is next to Godliness".

PRAYER FOR DAY TWO

Lord, let me be open to the peace and glory of the Season as I reflect on how I can prepare to know You.

Activity

Review the previous year. Do any people come to mind that you wish you had treated better? Make an effort to call, text, email or see them. No need to mention the past. Just bring them joy by saying "hello". As you brighten others' lives, you will also be brightening your soul.

PRAYER FOR DAY THREE

Lord, let me be of peace and comfort to my family, particularly in this Christmas season when tempers can fray and words can be spoken in anger.

Activity

Prepare a special treat for your family. This can be a favorite meal, a fancy dessert or maybe even a pretzel at the mall. As you feed your family with this special food, you are letting them know that they are special to you.

PRAYER FOR DAY FOUR

Lord, bless me with thoughts of Joy and Hope as we prepare to celebrate the Christ Child's birth.

Activity

Donate canned goods or clothes at a church, thrift store or shelter. Every effort we make to help the least of our brethren you do unto Him.

PRAYER FOR DAY FIVE

Lord, let me remember that angels bring us messages and relay hope. Let me always be ready to receive my angel's truth.

Activity

Reach out to bring a happy message to someone in your life. Although most people now text or email each other, take a different approach. Honor that special person with a good word from you in a letter or a card.

PRAYER FOR DAY SIX

Lord, let me celebrate this season with Joy and Peace and not forget the least of my friends, as You never forgot yours.

Activity

Think of someone that you have been meaning to call. If you are up to date on your connections, you are in a truly blessed place. Instead, think of someone that is experiencing an unusually hard time. Contact them and learn what it is that would make their life easier. Then do it. Baby sit the children; write a letter for them; buy them a book. Let them know you are a friend.

PRAYER FOR DAY SEVEN

Lord, please still my mind so that my heart may receive the message of the season.

Activity

Take a moment to pray. If possible, go somewhere quiet where you can be alone. I realize that for some people this may mean sitting in the car or even hiding in the bathroom. Find that place. And give yourself just five minutes (on the clock, don't cheat!) to think of absolutely nothing. Do not think about your to-do list, money concerns, the menu for dinner or anything else. Just give yourself some time to receive goodness from God.

PRAYER FOR DAY EIGHT

Lord, let me love my family and friends as you would. During this time, we commemorate the birth of your son, whom You sacrificed to save the world.

Activity

Lead your family in prayer. This can be as simple as all joining hands and reciting the "Our Father". This act of prayer can be done before a meal, first thing in the morning or the last thing before bed.

PRAYER FOR DAY NINE

Lord, let me appreciate the beauty around me. May the decorations of the Season serve to remind me of the beauty you have bestowed in all our hearts.

Activity

Make a plan for your Christmas decorations. Write down the plan so that when the time comes to decorate, you will have all the materials at hand and know exactly what goes where. You will not only be able to use the beauty of the decorations to remind you of God's gifts to us, but you should lower your stress significantly.

PRAYER FOR DAY TEN

Lord, let me love you unconditionally. Let me use the promise of Christ's birth to realize that you love all of us.

Activity

Take five minutes to pray to our Lord. Let him know how much you need him and how grateful you are that He is in your life.

PRAYER FOR DAY ELEVEN

Lord, let my heart focus on the good in all my neighbors and friends. Through the celebration of this season, You remind us that, even though your Son was born in humble beginnings, He rose to become the Savior of us all.

Activity

Do something nice for one of your neighbors. It doesn't matter which neighbor or what you do. Bring in their newspaper from the front lawn, bring their trashcan down to the street or up to the house. Call them and ask if they need anything the next time you venture to the store.

PRAYER FOR DAY TWELVE

Lord, let me not be distracted by the hustle and bustle of the season. Let me know I should not worry about tasks to be done and presents to be bought. Instead, I should relax and bask in your Light.

Activity

Make a list of everything you have to do to prepare for Christmas, both materially and spiritually. Include absolutely everything, from costumes for your child's play to decorating the tree. Once the list is complete, heave a big sigh of relief. Now that you know everything that has to be done, don't worry about it. Assign times and if possible, people to tasks and get prepared to check off your list. Note: it is important that you refrain from adding anything to your list. I know it's hard, but you want to keep your efforts simple. I would recommend buying a generic present or two, like chocolates or candles, that you can keep under the tree should a special need arise and another gift is required.

PRAYER FOR DAY THIRTEEN

Lord, let me humble myself as you have done in coming to this world as a babe in swaddling clothing.

Activity

Get down on your knees (if at all possible). Otherwise, take a seat. Perform this act in a quiet place. While you are on your knees, say the prayer above. Reflect on the gifts God has bestowed upon you and your family.

PRAYER FOR DAY FOURTEEN

Lord, let me understand that the simple life is the better life. It encompasses the only thing that matters, Your love.

Activity

Review your Christmas plans. Eliminate one to-do from that list. I guarantee that not everything on that list is a must-have. Learn that simplifying the season, even by just one little bit, you will be more relaxed and able to remember the "reason for the season".

PRAYER FOR DAY FIFTEEN

Lord, let me not give in to the temptation of excess. Let me remember that, as You were born, You embodied the humble state of love.

Activity

Dispose of five things in your home, office or garage. Give these to a charity, a friend or the trash heap. Even those these are just five things, the act of sharing or removing them from your home will give you peace. Things do not make us happy; the Lord's love does.

PRAYER FOR DAY SIXTEEN

Lord, let me strive to spread the word of love throughout the day, in each word I speak and in each action I take.

Activity

Write a letter to a loved one. This person can be a child, parent or friend. In this letter describe all of the reasons they are important to you. List all of the joy they have brought you and all of the light they have brought into your world. Then set aside this missive of love to read at the start of next year's advent season.

PRAYER FOR DAY SEVENTEEN

Lord, let me be honest with myself and recognize how I can act to reflect Your love.

Activity

Make (or buy) a meal for your neighbor, mother, child, shut-in, office mate. Food is always welcome. During this busy time, a ready-made meal will be truly appreciated.

PRAYER FOR DAY EIGHTEEN

Lord, let me appreciate the good you have given me. Let me carry this good with me throughout the day.

Activity

Start the day with something you enjoy. This can be a cup of coffee from the café down the street, a chocolate croissant, reading a chapter of a book you love or perhaps even saying a prayer. Then, as your day unfolds and challenges arise, reflect on the joy you experienced that morning.

PRAYER FOR DAY NINETEEN

Lord, let me carry your message of peace and tranquility with me as I move throughout the day.

Activity

Say aloud (or sing) one of the hymns in this book. Singing and reciting relax the body as you breathe in and out more deeply than usual.

PRAYER FOR DAY TWENTY

Lord, guide me to help those in need. Everyone deserves to feel your Joy.

Activity

Be sure to say, "Hi, have a nice day!" to at least five strangers today. These can be people at the grocery store, at the bus stop, or at church. Very often it is the tiniest kindness that change a person's outlook and bring an angel to their heart.

PRAYER FOR DAY TWENTY-ONE

Lord, let me lean on You and remember that you are always there to provide comfort.

Activity

Grab a piece of paper and pen (or sign on to your tablet or computer). Write your own prayer to our Lord. Try to express the gratitude you feel for knowing that He is always available to you. Keep this prayer and recite it today and every day until Christmas.

PRAYER FOR DAY TWENTY-TWO

Lord, help me reflect on Your love during this Christmas season that we may be filled with Your peace and joy.

Activity

Read a Bible verse that relates the story of Christ's birth. Imagine how you would have reacted had you been invited to the blessed event.

PRAYER FOR DAY TWENTY-THREE

Lord, let me be generous to others who are not generous to me.

Activity

Make homemade cards (or buy several from the Dollar store). Add a candy cane. Distribute these to the neighbors, your friends or a nursing home. Take donuts to a place you frequent: the office, a store (to treat the employees), to a school (for the teachers).

PRAYER FOR DAY TWENTY-FOUR

Lord, let me rejoice that you are here to bring Light and Love. Grant me the power to listen to your words.

Activity

Find a quiet place and read the bible verses included in this book. Reflect on the words and prepare your heart for December twenty-fifth by letting the joy of Christmas ring within.

PRAYER FOR DAY TWENTY-FIVE (ALSO DAY ONE OF THE CHRISTMAS CELEBRATION)

Lord, let me look upon your birth as the angels did with Hope and Joy.

Activity

The best way to celebrate Christ's birth is to surround yourself with love. hare a meal with friends, family or even strangers. Wish them a Merry Christmas. Rejoice that you are Christian and revel in God's love.

The Twelve Days of Christmas

TWELVE DAYS OF CHRISTMAS

The Twelve Days of Christmas is a festive period that is deeply rooted in Christian tradition, beginning on December 25th, Christmas Day, and concluding on January 5th, the eve of the Epiphany. Each day within this period holds its own special significance, often associated with various saints, feasts, and important events in Christian history. Some religions refer to this time period as Christmastide.

Why We Celebrate the Twelve Days of Christmas

The celebration of the Twelve Days of Christmas has its origins in the early Church, where it was seen as a way to fully appreciate and contemplate the mystery of the Incarnationâ€"God becoming man in the person of Jesus Christ. By stretching the celebration across twelve days, early Christians were able to meditate more deeply on the significance of Christâ€™s birth, rather than confining it to a single day.

In many cultures, the Twelve Days are marked by various customs and traditions, such as the giving of gifts, special meals, and communal gatherings. These customs are often designed to reinforce the spiritual themes of the season, such as generosity, gratitude, and the importance of community.

PRAYER FOR DAY TWO CHRISTMAS

CELEBRATION

Lord, as we remember the angels who proclaimed Your birth with songs of praise, fill our hearts with the same joy and wonder. Help us to lift our voices in worship and to spread peace and goodwill to all we meet. Let our lives be a reflection of the heavenly host's proclamation: Lord, let me rejoice that you are here to bring Light and Love. Grant me the power to listen to your words.

Activity

Sing Christmas carols that focus on the angels and their announcement of Jesus' birth. Consider visiting a neighbor or nursing home to spread the joy of Christmas through song.

Feast of St. Stephen:

Commemorates St. Stephen, the first Christian

martyr, known for his acts of charity and his courageous

faith.

PRAYER FOR DAY THREE

CHRISTMAS CELEBRATION

Lord, today we reflect on the humble circumstances of Jesus' birth. Teach us to find contentment in simplicity and to cherish the blessings we often take for granted. May we, like the shepherds, approach You with awe and reverence, rejoicing in the miracle of Christ's birth. Guide us to live in humility and service to others. Amen.

Activity

Make a simple nativity scene using craft supplies or items from around the house. As you assemble the scene, reflect on the humility of Jesus' birth and what it means for you today.

Feast of St. John the Evangelist:

Honors St. John, one of the Twelve Apostles and

the author of the Gospel of John..

PRAYER FOR DAY FOUR

CHRISTMAS CELEBRATION

Gracious God, as we think about where our treasure lies, help us to prioritize what truly matters. May our hearts be set on the things above, where true joy and fulfillment are found. Give us the wisdom to use our resources in ways that honor You and bless those in need. Lead us to be generous, compassionate, and mindful of Your will. Amen.

Activity

Set aside some time to declutter your home and gather items to donate to those in need. This is a practical way to shift your focus from material possessions to what truly matters—love and generosity.

Feast of the Holy Innocents:

Remembers the children killed by King Herod in his

attempt to eliminate the Christ child, recognizing their martyrdom.

PRAYER FOR DAY FIVE CHRISTMAS CELEBRATION

Lord Jesus, You are the Word made flesh, full of grace and truth. As we reflect on the mystery of Your Incarnation, may our hearts be filled with gratitude and wonder. Help us to see Your presence in our lives and to be faithful witnesses of Your love to the world. Strengthen our faith and deepen our understanding of Your divine purpose. Amen.

Activity

Spend time journaling about the significance of the Incarnation —God becoming flesh. Write down your thoughts on how Jesus' coming to earth has impacted your life.

Feast of St. Thomas Becket:

Commemorates St. Thomas Becket, Archbishop of Canterbury,

who was martyred in 1170 for defending the rights of the Church.

PRAYER FOR DAY SIX CHRISTMAS CELEBRATION

Lord, as the shepherds shared the good news of Jesus' birth, empower us to share the message of salvation with those around us. Give us courage to speak of Your love and to live in a way that draws others to You. May our words and actions reflect the hope and joy we find in Christ. Use us as instruments of Your peace and grace. Amen.

Activity

Share the story of Jesus' birth with someone who may not know it well. This could be a child, a friend, or someone in your community. Use a nativity storybook or your own words.

Feast of the Holy Family:

Celebrates the Holy Family of Jesus, Mary, and Joseph as a model

for all Christian families.

PRAYER FOR DAY SEVEN

CHRISTMAS CELEBRATION

Dear Lord, as the year draws to a close, we thank You for Your faithfulness through every moment. We lay before You our hopes, our fears, and our dreams for the coming year. Guide us in Your ways and grant us the wisdom to follow Your path. May we enter the New Year with hearts full of trust in Your goodness and plans for our lives. Amen.

Activity

Reflect on the year that is ending and how God has shown His favor in your life. Write down your blessings and thank God for His faithfulness as you prepare to welcome the New Year.

Feast of St. Sylvester:

Honors St. Sylvester I, Pope during the time of Emperor

Constantine and known for his role in the early Church.

PRAYER FOR DAY EIGHT

CHRISTMAS CELEBRATION

Lord, as we step into a new year, we pray for new beginnings in our lives. Renew our spirits and transform us into the people You created us to be. Help us to leave behind what hinders our walk with You and to embrace the newness of life found in Christ. Guide us in every decision and fill our days with Your presence. Amen.

Activity

Create a "New Beginnings" jar. Write down things you want to leave behind and new goals or resolutions for the upcoming year. Place the jar somewhere you can see it regularly as a reminder of your commitment to grow in Christ.

Solemnity of Mary, Mother of God:

Celebrates Mary's role as the mother of Jesus Christ and honors

her as the Mother of God.

PRAYER FOR DAY NINE

CHRISTMAS CELEBRATION

Loving Father, like Mary, who pondered the mysteries of Your plan in her heart, help us to take time to reflect on Your work in our lives. Teach us to listen to Your voice and to trust in Your timing. May we grow in faith and understanding, and may our hearts be open to the ways You are leading us. Give us the patience to wait on You and the wisdom to follow Your guidance. Amen.

Activity

Take time for quiet reflection. Find a peaceful spot, perhaps by a window with a view of nature, and meditate on the story of Jesus' birth and what it means to you personally. Write down any insights that come to you.

Feast of Basil the Great and Gregory Nazianzus:

Honors these two important bishops and theologians who

contributed significantly to Christian doctrine.

PRAYER FOR DAY TEN CHRISTMAS

CELEBRATION

Lord, as we think of the wise men who brought gifts to the Christ child, help us to offer You the best of ourselves—our time, talents, and treasures. May we give freely and joyfully, knowing that everything we have is a gift from You. Teach us to worship You with our whole hearts and to live in gratitude for the greatest gift of all, Jesus Christ. Amen

Activity

Give a gift to someone who may not be expecting it. This could be a small token of appreciation, a handmade item, or even your time. As you give, remember the wise men's gifts to Jesus and how we, too, can offer our best to Him.

Feast of the Holy Name of Jesus:

Focuses on the significance and reverence of the name of Jesus.

PRAYER FOR DAY ELEVEN

CHRISTMAS CELEBRATION

Lord, fill our hearts with Your peace as we move through this season. Help us to be thankful in all circumstances, trusting that You are in control and that Your plans for us are good. May Your peace rule in our hearts and overflow into our relationships with others. Let our lives be marked by thankfulness and contentment, rooted in Your love. Amen.

Activity

Spend time writing thank-you notes or making calls to people who have impacted your life in the past year. Express your gratitude and share the peace that comes from God's presence in your life.

Feast of Elizabeth Ann Seton:

Commemorates the first native-born American saint, known for

her role in founding the Catholic school system in the United States.

PRAYER FOR DAY TWELVE

CHRISTMAS CELEBRATION

Heavenly Father, as we reflect on the journey of the wise men, we pray for the guidance of Your light in our own lives. Help us to seek You diligently and to follow where You lead, even when the path is uncertain. May we rejoice in Your presence and share in the joy of knowing Christ. Guide us by Your light, and let our lives shine with the love of Jesus. Amen.

Activity

Create star-shaped ornaments or decorations to hang in your home. As you craft, talk with your family or friends about what it means to follow Jesus, the Light of the World, just as the wise men followed the star to find Him.

Twelfth Night (Eve of the Epiphany):

Marks the final day of the Twelve Days of Christmas,

leading into the Feast of the Epiphany, which celebrates

the visit of the Magi to the Christ child.

Angels and the Christmas Season

Part of our celebration of the birth of Christ includes remembrances of angels. Angels are part of the nativity scene. They are part of the celebration in the form of angels on top of Christmas trees, angel cookies, and angel decorations.

You may want to try some of the below activities to share your knowledge of angels with children, friends, and other family members.

ANGEL DOLL

Creating a simple, yet beautiful angel, using a doll and a paper plate for wings is a fun and easy craft project. Here's how you can make your own angel:

Materials Needed:

- **Doll:** Any small doll, preferably one with a fixed body (a Barbie-sized doll or a small plastic doll works well).

- **Paper Plate:** A standard-sized paper plate.

- **Scissors**

- **Glue:** Hot glue gun or craft glue.

- **Markers, Paint, or Crayons:** For decorating the wings.

- **Ribbon or Yarn:** For hanging the angel (optional).

- **Glitter, Stickers, or Other Decorations:** To embellish the wings (optional).

Step-by-Step Instructions:

1. Prepare the Doll:

- If your doll has any accessories (like hats or shoes) that might interfere with the angel's appearance, remove them.

- If desired, you can dress the doll in white or light-colored fabric to give it a more angelic appearance.

2. Create the Wings from the Paper Plate:

- Take the paper plate and fold it in half.

- Draw a wing shape on one side of the folded plate. The wings should be large enough to be proportional to the doll.

- Cut out the wing shape, making sure to keep the fold intact so that you end up with two symmetrical wings.

3. Decorate the Wings:

- Use markers, paint, or crayons to decorate the wings. You can draw feather patterns, add glitter for a sparkling effect, or use stickers to embellish the wings.

- If you want to create a layered look, you can cut smaller wing shapes from colored paper and glue them onto the paper plate wings.

4. Attach the Wings to the Doll:

- Once the wings are decorated and dry, apply a small amount of glue to the center fold of the wings.

• Press the glued center of the wings onto the back of the doll. Hold it in place until the glue sets. If you're using a hot glue gun, this should only take a few seconds.

5. Add a Halo (Optional):

• To create a halo, cut a small piece of ribbon or yarn and form it into a loop.

• Attach the loop to the top of the doll's head using glue, or if the doll has hair, you can tuck it in.

6. Attach a Hanging Loop (Optional):

• If you want to hang the angel, cut a length of ribbon or yarn.

• Glue the ends of the ribbon or yarn to the back of the doll's head or shoulders, ensuring it's long enough to hang from a tree or hook.

7. Final Touches:

• Check that the wings are securely attached and adjust them if necessary.

• You can add final decorations like tiny stars, additional glitter, or even a small ribbon bow on the angel's dress.

Displaying Your Angel:

• **Ornament:** If you added a hanging loop, your angel can be used as a Christmas tree ornament.

• **Tabletop Decoration:** Without the loop, your angel can be placed on a table or mantle as part of your holiday decor.

Creating this angel is a great way to repurpose an old doll and a simple paper plate into a meaningful and festive decoration. It's also a wonderful activity to do with children, allowing them to use their creativity while making something special for the holiday season.

PHOTO ANGEL

A perfect gift is an angel that displays a person's photograph.

Here are step-by-step instructions for creating this meaningful and personalized angel craft:

Materials Needed:

· **Drawing Paper or Cardstock:** For your angel drawing.

· **Pencils, Markers, Crayons, or Colored Pencils:** For drawing and coloring the angel.

· **Scissors**

· **Glue or Double-Sided Tape**

· **Photo of Someone You Love:** A small photo that can be cut and pasted onto the angel.

· **Optional Decorations:** Glitter, stickers, or any other embellishments.

Step-by-Step Instructions:

1. Draw the Angel:

- Start by drawing an angel on the paper. Begin with the head, drawing a simple circle for the face.

- Add the body by drawing a flowing robe that extends from the neck down to the bottom of the paper. The robe can be as simple or as detailed as you like.

- Draw the wings on either side of the body. Make them large enough to stand out, curving outward and upward from the shoulders.

- Add details to the face, such as eyes, a nose, and a smile. You can also draw a halo above the angel's head.

2. Color the Angel:

- Use your markers, crayons, or colored pencils to color in the angel.

- Choose soft, light colors for the robe and wings, or get creative and use bright, vibrant colors.

- Add shading or patterns to the robe and wings to give your angel more depth and character.

3. Cut Out the Photo:

- Take the photo of the person you love and carefully cut it out to fit the space you want to place it on the angel.

- If you plan to place the photo on the heart, cut it into a heart shape. If it's going on the wings, trim the edges so it fits nicely.

4. Paste the Photo onto the Angel:

- Decide whether you want to place the photo on the angel's wings or over the heart area.

- Apply glue or use double-sided tape on the back of the photo and carefully place it on the chosen spot on your angel.

- Press down gently to make sure the photo is securely attached.

5. Optional Decorations:

- If you like, you can add glitter around the wings or the halo to make your angel sparkle.

- You can also use stickers, rhinestones, or other embellishments to personalize your angel further.

6. Display Your Angel:

- Once the glue has dried and your angel is complete, display it in a special place.

- This angel can be hung on the wall, placed on your desk, or used as a holiday decoration.

Symbolism:

By pasting the photo of someone you love on the angel's wings or heart, you are symbolizing the protection and care that angels are believed to offer. This craft serves as a beautiful reminder of the love and connection you share with that person, making it not only a decorative piece but also a meaningful keepsake.

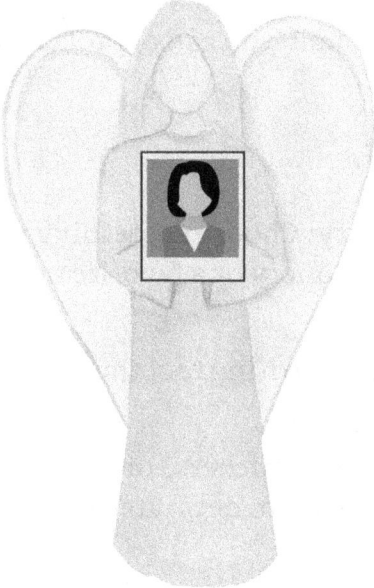

WRITE A LETTER TO YOUR ANGEL

Writing a letter to an angel can be a deeply personal and spiritual experience. It allows you to express your thoughts, feelings, and desires in a way that connects with your faith and sense of peace. Here's how you can approach writing such a letter:

Materials Needed:

- **Paper or Stationery:** Choose something that feels special, like a piece of nice stationery or a favorite notebook.

- **Pen or Pencil:** Use a writing tool that feels comfortable to you.

- **Optional:** Envelopes, stickers, or any other embellishments you might want to use to decorate your letter.

Step-by-Step Instructions:

1. Find a Quiet Space:

- Choose a quiet, peaceful place where you can focus without distractions. This could be a cozy corner of your home, a park, or any place where you feel at ease.

- Take a few deep breaths to clear your mind and center yourself. You might want to say a short prayer or meditate briefly to help set a calm and reflective mood.

2. Address Your Angel:

- Begin your letter by addressing the angel. You could start with "Dear Guardian Angel," "Dear Angel," or "To My Beloved Angel."

- If you feel connected to a specific angel, such as Archangel Michael or Gabriel, you can address them by name.

3. Express Your Thoughts and Feelings:

- Write about what is on your heart. You might want to share your worries, fears, hopes, or anything that's been on your mind.

- If you're seeking guidance, ask for it in your letter. Be honest and open about what you're going through and how you'd like the angel's help or support.

- You can also express gratitude for any blessings you've received or for the angel's presence in your life.

4. Ask for Protection and Guidance:

- If there are specific areas in your life where you need protection or guidance, mention them in your letter.

- For example, you might write, "Please guide me as I make this important decision," or "Watch over my loved ones and keep them safe."

5. Share Your Dreams and Desires:

- Feel free to share your dreams and desires with your angel. Writing them down can be a powerful way to articulate what you truly want.

- Whether it's a personal goal, a wish for someone else, or a general hope for the future, let your angel know.

6. Conclude with Love and Trust:

- End your letter with a note of love and trust. You might write something like, "Thank you for always being there for me," or "I trust in your guidance and love."

- You can sign your letter with your name, or simply with "With love" or "In faith."

7. Optional: Decorate Your Letter:

- If you like, you can decorate your letter with stickers, drawings, or symbols that are meaningful to you.

- You might also want to place the letter in an envelope and keep it in a special place, like a prayer box or a journal.

8. Reflect on Your Letter:

- After writing, take a moment to reflect on your words. Writing to an angel can be a therapeutic process, helping you to clarify your thoughts and feelings.

- You might choose to read the letter aloud, as if speaking

directly to the angel.

9. Keep or Release the Letter:

• You can keep the letter as a reminder of your connection with your angel, or you might choose to release it—by burying it, burning it, or tearing it up as a symbolic act of letting go and trusting in the angel's care.

Final Thoughts:

Writing a letter to an angel is a personal act of faith and expression. It's an opportunity to communicate with a spiritual presence that brings comfort, guidance, and protection. Whether you're asking for help, expressing gratitude, or simply sharing your thoughts, this practice can bring a sense of and connection to something greater than yourself.

Dear Guardian Angel,

Thank you for watching over me.

Love,

ANGEL FOOD CAKE

Feast on angel food cake as a remembrance of angels that are in our hearts.

Decorating an angel food cake to celebrate angels can be a delightful and symbolic activity. Here's how you can do it:

Materials Needed:

- **Angel Food Cake:** Store-bought or homemade.

- **Whipped Cream or Frosting:** Choose your favorite, such as vanilla or cream cheese frosting.

- **Edible Glitter or Shimmer Powder:** To add a heavenly sparkle.

- **White Chocolate Chips or Candy Melts:** For angelic accents.

- **Fresh Berries or Edible Flowers:** For a touch of color and natural beauty.

- **Angel Cake Topper (Optional):** You can find these at a baking supply store or make your own.

Step-by-Step Instructions:

1. Prepare Your Cake:

- Place your angel food cake on a cake stand or serving plate. Make sure the cake is completely cool if you've baked it yourself.

2. Frost the Cake:

- Use whipped cream or frosting to cover the entire cake. Angel food cake has a light and airy texture, so a light layer of frosting works best.

- Start by applying a thin crumb coat (a very light layer of frosting to seal in the crumbs), then add a slightly thicker layer for a smooth finish.

3. Add Edible Glitter or Shimmer Powder:

- Sprinkle edible glitter or shimmer powder over the frosting to give the cake a magical, angelic appearance.

- Focus on the top and sides of the cake, adding as much or as little as you like for the desired level of sparkle.

4. Decorate with White Chocolate:

- Melt white chocolate chips or candy melts according to the package instructions.

- Once melted, use a spoon to drizzle the white chocolate over the top of the cake, letting it cascade down the sides like delicate angelic ribbons.

- You can also pipe the white chocolate into angel wing shapes on parchment paper, let them harden, and then place them on top of the cake for an added angelic touch.

5. Add Fresh Berries or Edible Flowers:

- Gently place fresh berries or edible flowers around the base of the cake and on the top. Blueberries, raspberries, and strawberries work well, as do small white or pastel-colored edible flowers like pansies or violets.

- These natural elements symbolize the beauty and purity often associated with angels.

6. Place an Angel Topper (Optional):

- If you have an angel cake topper, carefully place it in the center of the cake. This adds a focal point that ties the theme together.

- Alternatively, you can create a simple angel topper by cutting out an angel shape from cardstock, attaching it to a toothpick or skewer, and inserting it into the cake.

7. Serve and Celebrate:

- Your decorated angel food cake is now ready to serve! This cake not only looks divine but also tastes light and fluffy, perfect for celebrating the presence of angels.

- As you enjoy the cake, take a moment to reflect on the significance of angels and their role in your life. You might even say a prayer or share a story about angels with your loved ones.

Final Touch:

This angel food cake, adorned with sparkles, chocolate, and natural beauty, serves as a sweet reminder of the grace and presence of angels in our lives. Whether for a special occasion or just as a treat to celebrate faith, this cake is sure to be a hit.

ALUMINUM FOIL ANGELS

Create aluminum foil angels to hang on your Christmas tree. Their shining presence will enhance the festive appearance of your house.

Materials Needed:

- **Aluminum Foil:** A roll of standard kitchen aluminum foil.

- **Scissors:** For cutting the foil.

- **Pipe Cleaners:** Silver, white, or gold (optional, for added detail).

- **String or Ribbon:** To hang the angels on the tree.

- **Glue:** To attach the string or ribbon.

- **Markers or Paint:** For adding facial features (optional).

- **Beads or Small Buttons:** For the angel's head (optional).

Step-by-Step Instructions:

1. Cut the Aluminum Foil:

- Start by cutting a square piece of aluminum foil, approximately 6 inches by 6 inches. You can adjust the size based on how large you want your angels to be.

2. Create the Angel's Body:

- Take the square of foil and fold it in half diagonally to create a triangle.

- Gently scrunch the foil along the bottom of the triangle to form the angel's body, leaving the top part loose for the wings.

- Shape the body by pinching and molding the foil until you're satisfied with the form. The bottom should be slightly rounded.

3. Form the Wings:

- With the top part of the foil still loose, carefully spread out the two top corners to create the angel's wings. Fan them out slightly to give them a more wing-like appearance.

- You can also fold the wings back and forth like an accordion for a more textured look.

4. Add the Angel's Head (Optional):

- If you want to add a head, take a small bead or button and glue it to the top of the angel's body, right in the center where the wings meet.

- For a more finished look, you can cover the bead with a small piece of foil, leaving a smooth surface.

5. Attach the String or Ribbon:

- Cut a small piece of string or ribbon, about 4-6 inches long, depending on how you want your angel to hang.

- Fold the string or ribbon into a loop, then attach it to the back of the angel's head or the top of the body using glue.

- Let the glue dry completely before handling the angel further.

6. Optional Details:

- You can add facial features to your angel using a marker or paint. A simple dot for the eyes and a small smile can give your angel a charming expression.

- If you have pipe cleaners, you can twist them into halos or additional decorative elements for your angels. Attach these with a bit of glue.

7. Hang Your Angels:

- Once your angels are complete, they're ready to be hung on your Christmas tree. Their shiny, reflective surface will catch the light and add a festive glow to your tree.

- You can also use these foil angels to decorate other parts of your home, such as hanging them in windows or from door frames.

Final Touch:

These aluminum foil angels are not only a beautiful addition to your Christmas decorations but also a meaningful symbol of the season. Their shining presence on your tree will remind you of the joy and light that angels bring to the world, enhancing the festive spirit in your home.

CLOTHESPIN ANGEL

Crafting a clothespin angel is a fun and simple project that can add a charming, homemade touch to your holiday decorations. Here's how you can create your own clothespin angel:

Materials Needed:

- **Wooden Clothespin:** Standard size.
- **White Acrylic Paint:** For painting the clothespin.
- **Paintbrush:** For applying the paint.
- **Gold Pipe Cleaner:** For making the halo.
- **Paper Doily:** For the angel's wings.
- **Scissors:** For cutting the doily.
- **Glue or Hot Glue Gun:** To attach the wings and halo.
- **Optional Decorations:** Glitter, small gems, or ribbon.

Step-by-Step Instructions:

1. Paint the Clothespin:

- Begin by painting the entire wooden clothespin white. This will form the body of your angel.
- Apply a smooth, even coat of paint. You may need to apply a second coat for full coverage.
- Allow the paint to dry completely before proceeding to the next step.

2. Create the Halo:

- Take a gold pipe cleaner and cut a small piece, about 4 inches long.

- Form a loop with one end of the pipe cleaner to create the halo. The loop should be about the size of a dime.
- Twist the ends of the pipe cleaner to secure the loop, leaving a straight tail to attach to the clothespin.
- Bend the tail of the pipe cleaner at a right angle, so it can be glued to the back of the clothespin's "head."

3. Attach the Halo:

- Apply a small amount of glue to the back of the clothespinâ€™s upper section (the head area).
- Press the straight end of the pipe cleaner halo into the glue, positioning the halo above the top of the clothespin.
- Hold it in place until the glue sets, or use a hot glue gun for a quicker bond.

4. Make the Wings:

- Take a paper doily and fold it in half.
- Cut out two wing shapes from the folded doily. The wings should be roughly the same size as the clothespinâ€™s length.
- Once cut, unfold the doily wings and adjust them to ensure they are symmetrical and even.

5. Attach the Wings:

- Apply glue to the center of the wings, where the fold is.
- Position the wings on the back of the clothespin, just below the halo.
- Press the wings onto the clothespin, holding them in place until the glue sets. Ensure that the wings are centered and fanned out nicely.

6. Optional Decorations:

- If desired, you can add glitter to the wings or the body of the angel for a bit of sparkle.
- You can also glue small gems or tie a ribbon around the "waist" of the clothespin for additional decoration.

Final Touch:

- Allow all the glue and paint to dry completely before displaying your clothespin angel.
- These angels can be used as ornaments for your Christmas tree, decorations around your home, or even as thoughtful, homemade gifts.

Your clothespin angel is now complete! This simple and delightful craft can be enjoyed by crafters of all ages and adds a special touch to your holiday decor.

ANGEL GREETING CARDS

Create cards with pictures of angels on the front. There are many sites on the internet that provide free pictures for coloring and decorating.

Creating Angel Christmas cards is a delightful craft that can be shared with family and friends during the holiday season. Hereâ€™s how to make your own beautiful angel-themed cards:

Materials Needed:

- **Blank Cards or Cardstock:** Choose a size that fits your preference (typically 5x7 inches).
- **Colored Paper:** Various colors for the angels.
- **Markers, Colored Pencils, or Crayons:** For adding details and color.
- **Glue Stick or Liquid Glue:** To attach the paper pieces.
- **Scissors:** For cutting shapes and designs.
- **Stickers or Decorative Items:** Optional, for embellishing the cards.
- **Glitter (optional):** For adding sparkle to the angels.

Step-by-Step Instructions:

1. Prepare the Card Base:

- Start with your blank card or cardstock. If using cardstock, fold it in half to create the card base.
- Ensure the fold is sharp by running your finger or a ruler along the edge.

2. Design the Angel:

- **Cut Out the Angel Body:** From the colored paper, cut out a simple angel shape. You can create a basic body using a large circle for the head and an oval for the body.
- **Wings:** Cut out two wing shapes from another piece of colored paper. These can be heart-shaped or elongated ovals for a traditional look.
- **Halo:** Cut a thin strip of gold or yellow paper for the halo. Form it into a circle and glue it at the top of the angel's head.

3. Assemble the Angel:

. Glue pieces of the angel to the card

4. Add a Greeting:

Inside the card, write a heartfelt message, such   as, "Wishing you Peace and Joy this Christmas."

5. Final Touches:

- Review your card and add any additional decorations as desired, such as borders or festive drawings around the edges.
- Allow any glue or decorations to dry completely before handling the card further.

Tips:

- **Make a Set:** Create several angel cards to give to friends and family, sharing your angelic designs.
- **Personalize:** Encourage kids to make their own unique designs and messages for a personal touch.
- **Use Different Styles:** Try different angel designs, such as

traditional, cartoonish, or abstract styles.

Your handmade Angel Christmas cards will spread joy and warmth during the holiday season, bringing smiles to those who receive them!

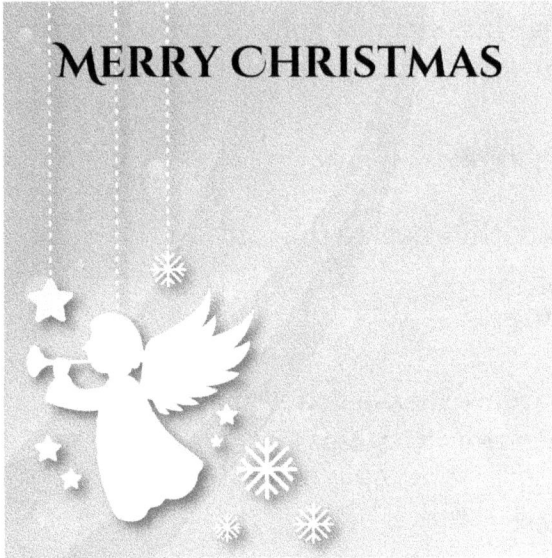

ANGEL GIFT WRAP

Paste pictures of angels on the presents you wrap. These can be angels you have drawn and colored or cut-outs from craft stores.

Decorating your presents with angel images adds a special, heartfelt touch that enhances the joy of gift-giving. Whether you use your own drawings or cut-outs from a craft store, these angel decorations will make your gifts stand out. Here's how to do it:

Materials Needed:

- **Wrapping Paper:** Your choice of festive paper.

- **Tape:** Clear or double-sided.

- **Scissors:** For cutting paper and images.

- **Glue Stick or Craft Glue:** To attach the angel pictures.

- **Angel Images:** Drawn and colored by you, or cut-outs from a craft store.

- **Markers, Crayons, or Colored Pencils:** If drawing your own angels.

- **Ribbon or Bow:** Optional, for additional decoration.

Step-by-Step Instructions:

1. Wrap the Presents:

- Begin by wrapping your gifts with your chosen wrapping paper. Use clear tape to secure the paper neatly around the present.

- If you want to add ribbon or a bow, you can do that after

attaching the angel pictures.

2. Prepare the Angel Images:

• If Drawing Your Own Angels:

- ◦ Use a piece of white or colored paper to draw your angel. Outline the shape of the angel, including wings, a halo, and any other details you like.

- ◦ Color the angel using markers, crayons, or colored pencils. Be creative with the colors, making your angel vibrant and cheerful.

- ◦ Carefully cut out the angel image once it's drawn and colored.

• If Using Store-Bought Cut-Outs:

- ◦ Select your favorite angel cut-outs from a craft store. These might be made from paper, stickers, or even felt.

- ◦ If the cut-outs are not already adhesive, use scissors to trim any excess paper or material around the edges for a clean look.

3. Attach the Angel Images:

- Decide where on the wrapped gift you'd like to place the angel image. The center of the top side is usually the best spot.

- Apply glue to the back of your angel image, whether it's hand-drawn or a cut-out. If you're using craft glue, apply a thin, even layer to avoid wrinkling the paper.

- Press the angel image firmly onto the wrapped present, smoothing out any bubbles or wrinkles. Hold it in place for a few seconds to ensure it sticks well.

4. Add Finishing Touches:

- If you want to add more decorations, consider placing a ribbon or bow around the present, taking care not to cover the angel.

- You can also write a small message or the recipient's name near the angel to make the gift even more personalized.

5. Display and Gift:

- Once your angels are securely attached and any additional decorations are in place, your present is ready to be gifted.

- Place the gift under the Christmas tree, where the angel-adorned wrapping will add to the festive atmosphere.

Final Thought:

Decorating your presents with angels adds a meaningful, personal touch that reflects the spirit of the season. Each gift will not only be beautifully wrapped but also carry a message of peace, protection, and love, making your holiday celebrations even more special.

ANGEL LANTERNS

Here are step-by-step instructions for creating Angel Lanterns using paper or glass decorated with angel designs to illuminate your space:

Materials Needed:

For Paper Lanterns:

- Colored or white cardstock or construction paper
- Scissors
- Glue or double-sided tape
- Angel-themed stickers or cut-outs
- LED tealight candles (for safety)
- String or ribbon (optional, for hanging)
- Ruler
- Pencil

Instructions:

1. **Prepare the Paper:**

   ◦ Choose a piece of cardstock or construction paper in your desired color. White or pastel colors work well for a soft angelic look.
2. **Cut the Paper:**

   ◦ Using a ruler and pencil, measure and mark a rectangle (e.g., 10 inches tall and 6 inches wide).
   ◦ Cut out the rectangle carefully.

3. **Create the Lantern Shape:**

- On the shorter sides (6 inches), mark 1 inch in from the edge at the top and bottom.
- Draw lines connecting the top and bottom marks, creating flaps on each side. Cut along these lines to create the flaps.

4. **Decorate the Lantern:**

- Use angel-themed stickers, cut-outs, or draw angel designs directly onto the paper.
- You can also create angel wing shapes on a separate piece of paper, cut them out, and glue them to the sides of the lantern.

5. **Assemble the Lantern:**

- Fold the paper to create a cylindrical shape. Overlap the flaps and use glue or double-sided tape to secure them in place.
- Make sure the bottom is securely attached so it can hold the LED tealight.

6. **Add Lighting:**

- Place an LED tealight candle inside the lantern.

7. **Finishing Touches:**

- If desired, attach a string or ribbon to the top for hanging, or leave it as a tabletop decoration.

Tips:

- Experiment with different shapes and sizes for your lanterns.
- Consider using translucent paper for paper lanterns to allow more light to shine through.
- For a magical effect, place your lanterns in a dimly lit room or outside at night to see the angel designs glow.

Enjoy creating your beautiful **Angel Lanterns** to illuminate your space with a heavenly touch!

ANGEL WREATH

Craft a wreath featuring angels using various materials like fabric, paper, or natural elements.

Here are step-by-step instructions for crafting a beautiful Angel Wreath using various materials like fabric, paper, or natural elements:

Materials Needed:

- **Wreath Base:**
  - Wire wreath frame (12-16 inches) or a foam wreath base
- **Angel Decorations:**
  - Angel-themed ornaments or figures (plastic, fabric, or paper)
  - Angel cut-outs or printed images
- **Fabric or Ribbon:**
  - Tulle, felt, or cotton fabric in angelic colors (white, gold, pastel)
  - Ribbons in complementary colors for accents
- **Natural Elements (Optional):**
  - Pinecones, dried flowers, twigs, or greenery (like pine branches or holly)
- **Adhesives:**
  - Hot glue gun and glue sticks
  - Craft glue (for paper)
- **Scissors**
- **Wire or Twine:**
  - For hanging the wreath
- **Embellishments (Optional):**
  - Glitter, beads, or sequins for added sparkle

Instructions:

Step 1: Prepare the Wreath Base

1. **Choose Your Base:**
   - Select a wire or foam wreath frame as your base.
   - If using a foam base, you may want to wrap it in fabric or ribbon first for a finished look.

Step 2: Create the Angels

1. **Fabric Angels:**

   - Cut fabric into angel shapes or use a pattern to create angel figures.
   - Use different fabrics to create variety (e.g., tulle for wings and felt for bodies).
   - You can also use pre-made fabric angel ornaments.

2. **Paper Angels:**

   - Print or draw angel shapes on cardstock or colored paper.
   - Cut them out carefully.
   - Decorate them with glitter, markers, or stickers.

3. **Natural Element Angels (Optional):**

   - Use small pinecones or twigs to create a rustic angel figure.
   - Glue fabric wings to the pinecone or arrange twigs in the shape of an angel.

Step 3: Assemble the Wreath

1. **Arrange Your Decorations:**

- Lay out the angel decorations and any natural elements around the wreath base to find the best arrangement.
- Space them evenly and balance the colors and shapes.

2. **Attach the Angels:**

- Use a hot glue gun to attach the fabric or paper angels securely to the wreath base.
- If using natural elements, glue them in place around the angels for a cohesive look.

3. **Add Fabric and Ribbons:**

- Cut pieces of fabric or ribbon to tie around the wreath, creating bows or cascading pieces.
- Secure the fabric or ribbon with glue, or tie them in knots around the wreath for added texture.

Step 4: Add Embellishments

1. **Enhance the Wreath:**
   - Sprinkle glitter or add sequins to give your wreath a magical sparkle.
   - Attach small beads or embellishments to the angels or fabric pieces for added detail.

Step 5: Create a Hanging Mechanism

1. **Attach Wire or Twine:**
   - Cut a piece of wire or twine long enough to create a loop for hanging.
   - Attach it to the top of the wreath by twisting it around the frame or gluing it in place.

Step 6: Display Your Angel Wreath

1. **Find the Perfect Spot:**

- Hang your angel wreath on your front door, wall, or above a mantel to showcase your beautiful creation.
- Enjoy the festive spirit it brings to your home!

Tips:

- Customize your wreath with colors and materials that match your home decor or the season.
- Consider adding a personal touch, such as a family photo or a meaningful quote about angels.
- If making this craft with children, supervise them closely with hot glue and sharp scissors.

Creating an Angel Wreath is a wonderful way to celebrate the season and add a touch of heavenly charm to your home! Enjoy your crafting experience!

ACKNOWLEDGEMENT

If you liked this book, you might like some of my other books. You can join my mailing list by dropping by my website or if you have any comments, shoot me a note at authorkarenshockley@gmail.com. I am always happy to hear from people who've read my work. I try to answer every email I receive.

Please write a short review for me on Amazon. I greatly appreciate any kind words, even one or two sentences go a long way. The number of reviews a book receives greatly improves how well a book does on Amazon.

Author's Web Page:

https://karens-words.mailchimpsites.com

ABOUT THE AUTHOR

Karen Kazimer Shockley

Karen Kazimer Shockley is a devoted Christian author with a passion for sharing her faith through storytelling. With a diverse collection of books that range from heartwarming Christian children's stories to inspiring clean romances, Karen brings her love for Christ to every page. Her writing reflects her deep commitment to spreading messages of love, hope, and faith to readers of all ages. Whether crafting tales of young believers or weaving romantic narratives grounded in Christian values, Karen's work continues to inspire and uplift her audience.

BOOKS BY THIS AUTHOR

I Know Jesus Loves Me: In Every Way, On Every Day

Your child will love looking at the pictures that show how Jesus loves them.

Early readers will enjoy the simple words that accompany the pictures.

Truly a wonderful way to bring Jesus into their lives.

Dive into the heartwarming world of 'I Know Jesus Loves Me,' a captivating children's book filled with sweet illustrations and enchanting poems that gently guide young hearts to understand the boundless love of God. Through each page, embark on a delightful journey where colorful images and poetic verses come together to weave a reassuring tapestry of love, acceptance, and joy. Perfect for bedtime stories or quiet moments, this enchanting book is a treasure trove that nurtures the spiritual growth of young minds, instilling a profound understanding of the eternal love that surrounds them. 'I Know Jesus Loves Me' is more than a book; it's a heartfelt embrace that whispers the timeless message of divine love to every child's soul.

Easter Devotional: 40 Days Of Verses And Prayers For Lent

Welcome the spirit of Easter with open hearts and minds! As we embrace this joyous occasion, let us delve into the rich tapestry of biblical verses that illuminate its profound significance. From the resurrection of Christ to the promise of new beginnings, each verse carries with it a message of hope, renewal, and divine love.

Join us in a journey of reflection and meditation, as we ponder the deeper meanings behind these timeless scriptures. Let every word resonate within you, guiding you towards a deeper understanding of faith and gratitude.

And as we immerse ourselves in the beauty of these sacred texts, let us also lift our voices in prayer, expressing our gratitude and joy for the blessings bestowed upon us. Together, let us celebrate the miracle of Easter and the boundless grace it brings into our lives.

This Easter season, may the verses of the Bible fill your heart with peace, inspire your soul, and renew your spirit. Join us in this uplifting exploration of faith, and let the words of scripture guide you towards a brighter tomorrow.

Angels, Saints, And Spirits: Through Her Own Experience

Do you feel like you can't explain many events that happen in your daily life? Karen feels this way too. In Angels, Saints, and Spirits, Karen takes you through real-life experiences that seem to be precipitated by spiritual events. As you listen to her stories, you, too, will be able to identify times in your life when the unexplained has no apparent rhyme or reason. It just happens.

That is the time to look beyond yourself and into the world of a greater power.

The events depicted in this book helped solidify Karen's belief in Christianity. As you listen to these stories, she hopes that you, too, can understand those times when God has intervened in a most special way.

www.ingramcontent.com/pod-product-compliance
Lightning Source LLC
Chambersburg PA
CBHW061747020426
42331CB00006B/1387